IMAGES
of America

TAMPA
UNION STATION

As a general rule, passenger trains that ran to Tampa Union Station backed in. Trains were turned on a nearby wye prior to their arrival at the station, necessitating patience on the part of both passengers and train crews eager to get to their final destination. This part of the Tampa Union Station experience was aptly captured on April 12, 1974, when photographer Fred Clark Jr. shot this picture of two trainmen at the rear of an Amtrak train arriving at the terminal. (Fred Clark Jr.)

IMAGES
of America

TAMPA
UNION STATION

Jackson McQuigg

ARCADIA

First published 1998
Copyright © Jackson McQuigg, 1998

ISBN 0-7524-0461-X

Published by Arcadia Publishing,
an imprint of Tempus Publishing, Inc.
2 Cumberland Street, Charleston SC 29401.
Printed in Great Britain

Library of Congress Cataloging-in-Publication Data applied for

Contents

Introduction

"The Tampa union station will be opened to the public at 6 o' clock
tomorrow morning. Everything is being placed in readiness today,
under the direction of Stationmaster Harry Love."
—The Tampa *Times*, May 14, 1912

1912. William Howard Taft was president of the United States. The world's first commercial airline flight—made by pilot Tony Jannus's St. Petersburg-Tampa Airboat Line—was still two years away. Model Ts and streetcars roamed Tampa's avenues and boulevards, forced to share the road with wagons and carriages, holdovers from a previous time. The 320-room Hillsboro Hotel would open downtown at Florida and Twiggs Streets that year, but it was the dedication of another place of lodging 21 years earlier—the railroad-owned Tampa Bay Hotel—which had first marked the city's coming of age.

Completed in 1891 at a cost of $3 million, the Tampa Bay Hotel was the capstone of a building spree initiated by financier and Southern Express Company owner Henry B. Plant the decade before. On January 22, 1884, the Plant-controlled South Florida Railroad completed its planned line into Tampa. Seventy-five miles of right-of-way, roadbed, and track—linking Tampa to an existing Plant System railroad line at Kissimmee—were fashioned through acres of rough-hewn woodland and palmetto scrub. A state charter for the South Florida Railroad—purchased by Plant at a fire sale price after its previous owner could not secure the financing to build the line—was most generous; it granted Plant a whopping 13,840 acres of real estate for each of the 75 miles of line.

Tampa would be incorporated one year after the arrival of the Plant System. Seven years later, Plant hoped that the lavish 511-room hotel would transform Tampa from a mere town into a *destination*, specifically a destination for the wealthy. And there was reason to think that such an undertaking would be successful. Across the state, railroad baron Henry Flagler was creating his own string of railroad hotels, a creation which began with the opening of the Flagler-owned Ponce de Leon Hotel in St. Augustine in May 1887; the Tampa Bay Hotel was Plant's answer to the doings of his rival.

Plant's hotel was destined to become a business failure, though the beautiful minaret-topped building later thrived in a new incarnation, Plant Hall on the University of Tampa campus— a role that it has played since 1933. Tampa thrived, too, and soon boasted a second railroad. The

Florida Central & Peninsular Railroad opened a line into town on May 1, 1890, and by 1893 had a system that stretched from Tampa to Savannah, Georgia, and beyond.

The Florida Central & Peninsular became part of the Seaboard Air Line Railway upon the creation of that railroad corporation in 1900; the Plant System was absorbed into the Atlantic Coast Line Railroad in 1905. Still another railroad, the Tampa Northern, was incorporated in 1906 as a subsidiary of the Atlanta, Birmingham & Atlantic Railroad; in 1912, its dreams of becoming a direct route from Atlanta to Tampa had been dashed by the bankruptcy of its parent company; that year, the Seaboard Air Line bought the railroad company, which had only gotten as far north as Brooksville.

It would be these three railroad companies—the Atlantic Coast Line, the Seaboard Air Line, and the Tampa Northern—that would front the $250,000 needed to build Tampa Union Station at Nebraska and Twiggs Streets downtown, under the auspices of the Tampa Union Station Company. On the day that the city's afternoon newspaper, the *Times*, let its readers know that everything was "being placed in readiness" at the station, Coast Line and Seaboard agents prepared to move their operations from separate passenger stations—at Polk and Tampa Streets, and Florida Avenue at Whiting Street, respectively—into the new building which would serve them jointly.

For the next 72 years, Tampa Union Station would serve as the city's main passenger station. Through its doors passed folks from all walks of life, and from every possible background: from World War II draftees heading off to training camps, to college kids leaving home and parents for the first time, from movie stars of the 1930s to "flower children" of the 1960s. At the beginning of its career, Tampa Union Station maintained separate waiting rooms, dictated by Jim Crow laws; yet it survived to see black Tampans departing from beneath its eaves aboard trains bound for Washington, D.C., and the epic 1963 March on Washington.

Through the years, the building would be no stranger to dramatic change. Steam locomotives ruled the rails during Tampa Union Station's early days. But a harbinger of things to come appeared at the facility's doorsteps on December 16, 1938. On that date the station witnessed its first diesel-electric–powered passenger train, the west coast section of the Seaboard Air Line *Orange Blossom Special*. The first all streamlined train to serve the station, Seaboard's *Silver Meteor*, would appear soon thereafter, on February 6, 1939.

The building witnessed its corporate parents merge and evolve over time—from Seaboard Air Line Railway's receivership and subsequent reorganization as the Seaboard Air Line Rail*road* in the 1940s, to the 1967 merger of the Seaboard and its rival, Atlantic Coast Line. Tampa Union Station served on through the dissolution of the once-mighty Pullman Company on December 31, 1968, and the creation of Amtrak on May 1, 1971, scarcely noticing that Uncle Sam was thereafter running the trains which called at its platforms.

Many of the stories which grew out of its long career are colorful. Tom Russell, a railroad conductor who put in decades of service with the Seaboard Air Line, Seaboard Coast Line, and Amtrak, recalls an incident which took place at Tampa Union Station in the 1950s involving the New York Yankees, fresh from their completion of spring training at St. Petersburg. One of the team's star players, Mickey Mantle, had just had major, well-publicized knee surgery.

The team was traveling on several cars which had been leased from the railroad and the Pullman Company. The equipment had traveled from St. Pete to Tampa in a special move; the cars would later be attached to the rear of a scheduled passenger train (though, of course, kept "off limits" to common folk). "The cars carrying the Yankees had come in from St. Pete, and many of the players had already been drinking—they had a send-off party for them over there, you see. There was going to be a one or two hour layover at Tampa Union Station before the cars were put on the back of the *Palmland*, going north." So some of the players decided that drinking would help pass the time.

"Billy Martin, Mickey Mantle, and Hank Bower came up to me. They were looking to go get drunk. I sent them over to a bar across the street, and they came back with a package." Russell was to later regret his hospitality.

"A little later on, Mickey Mantle came out into the vestibule of one of the cars, wearing nothing but his damned Jockey shorts, horse-playing with some of the other guys on the team." Mantle was totally soused. "I mean, here he was horse-playing, and he was still fresh out of *knee surgery*! . . . Then, all of a sudden, he lost his balance and fell down the steps of the car and onto the station platform. And there wasn't a damn thing that me or any of the other guys from the train crew that were around could do to get there fast enough to catch him. He just fell. And that whole trip, I thought, 'oh, Lord. He's gone and trashed those *million-dollar knees*!'"

The era of ballplayers traveling by rail was long over by the time Tampa Union Station closed its doors to the public in 1984. By then, the proud structure was suffering from decades of neglect—in part brought about by the shifting loyalties of the traveling public. DC-9s and interstate highways were now the modes of transport favored by most going to and from Tampa; with Amtrak having moved out and into a temporary facility adjacent the building's platforms, Union Station was all but a forgotten relic which lay dormant on the edge of Ybor City.

Happily, a group of local preservationists never gave up on the station's future. They formed a not-for-profit group called Tampa Union Station Preservation & Redevelopment and provided for the station's salvation. Ultimately, their efforts would be brought to fruition by the cash support of groups such as the Florida Department of Transportation, the Florida Department of State, the City of Tampa, Hillsborough County, Amtrak, the National Trust for Historic Preservation, and Tampa Preservation, Inc., as well as no-interest purchase financing from CSX Transportation, the corporate descendant of the building's original owners. Other benefactors came out in force to help, too; Nationsbank, the *Tampa Tribune*, WFLA Channel 8, and many other companies and individuals all did more than their share to make the dream of a restored, functional, Tampa Union Station a reality.

The two-year, $2.1-million restoration and renovation of Tampa Union Station and its 1998 reopening have given the facility a new lease on life, and it may stand on the threshold of a renaissance in rail passenger service. In its next decades, the building could perhaps witness the arrival and departure of sleek commuter trains and high-speed, cross-state and interstate trains as different from today's rail travel as the first streamliner was from its steam-hauled predecessors. The rising and ebbing flows of government transportation monies will ultimately tell. Thus, as Harry Love's ultimate successor as stationmaster at Tampa Union Station, Amtrak Tampa station agent Doug Rutledge, unlocks the front doors of Union Station each new morning, one thing is for certain: Tampa Union Station is back, ready for a new century of service—and whatever it might bring.

Acknowledgments

One doesn't have to look far to find heroes. And so it has been with this book project.

The concept for this book was first discussed by the Historical Resources Committee of Tampa Union Station Preservation & Redevelopment (TUSP&R) in late 1995. I had nearly completed a book for the North Carolina Transportation Museum at Historic Spencer Shops, *History on Steel Wheels*; the thought was that perhaps I could pursue a Tampa Union Station book immediately on the heels of that work, creating ample time prior to the rededication of Tampa Union Station for researching such a work. The timetable for the restoration project was not yet set, however, and the renovation project—which has somewhat led a "Perils of Pauline" existence for much of its life-span—fell into jeopardy soon after our first discussions. A book about the history and restoration of Tampa Union Station wasn't feasible unless a restoration could actually take place.

In summer 1997, Jim Dunn of Arcadia Publishing approached my father, John McQuigg, a TUSP&R board member and its past president, about the publishing house's interest in doing books on historical Florida subjects. All agreed that a book about Tampa Union Station just might work, and with the timetable for the restoration by then assured, one thing led to another, and soon the concept for a book about the station was once again back on track.

However, to ensure that this book was published in time for the rededication of the station, we had to work efficiently. My father was not only instrumental in promoting the concept for this book to TUSP&R's board, but he also functioned as a researcher, digging through old city directories and bookshelves at the Tampa-Hillsborough County Public Library in downtown Tampa, making phone calls, and running errands, all at a moment's notice. I am further grateful for the support that Len Tria, president of TUSP&R, and Jim Shephard, its project director, lent to this project. Both played key roles in bringing *Images of America: Tampa Union Station* from concept to reality.

But perhaps the biggest heroes of them all to this project are the individuals and archival institutions which shared their collections with us—and did so on a very timely basis. Jim Herron, Fred Clark, and Joe Oates led the way on this front; I am also very grateful to Larry Goolsby, Andy Healy, August Staebler, Jim Shephard, Dud Goodwin, Roberta Niesz, Frank Ardrey, and M.D. McCarter. Barbara Sharkey of Amtrak in Tampa asked her fellow employees throughout the Amtrak system in the Sunshine State to share photos for this project, while architect Tom Hammer of Rowe Architects came through with photos and plans of the building in record time. George Cott of Chroma, Inc., Cliff Black and Steven Taubenkibel of Amtrak Public Affairs, the Atlantic Coast Line and Seaboard Air Line Railroads Historical Society, Cynthia Gandee of the Henry B. Plant Museum, Tina Russo of the Tampa-Hillsborough County Public Library, Art Bagley of the Merl Kelce Library at the University of Tampa, Tammy Galloway, Michael Rose, and Kathy Harmer of the Atlanta History Center, and Paul Camp of the University of South Florida Library Special Collections Department all provided invaluable assistance and great photographs to this book project.

Earlier, Tom Kemp and Paul Camp of the University of South Florida Special Collections Department and Martha Briggs of the Newberry Library (which is home to the Pullman Company archives) played instrumental roles in the preservation of several cartons of documents rescued from the building. Records dating back as far as the 1920s from the Seaboard Air Line, Atlantic Coast Line, Tampa Union Station Company, and the Pullman Company lay languishing in Tampa Union Station for decades until their removal by volunteers from TUSP&R's Historical Resources Committee in August 1995. TUSP&R found homes for these records and saw to their preservation thanks to the helpfulness and interest of these two fine institutions.

And finally, I am deeply indebted to my friends Kim Blass and John Patterson for serving as reviewers of early drafts of the photo caption text which appears on these pages.

Thank you all, very much.

One
Decline

Here is Tampa Union Station in an early-1970s postcard view. Except for one scrawny remnant, the palm trees are completely gone from the front lawn; other landscaping grows wild. The original, historic outdoor street lamps have long since quit working, so a modern street lamp has been erected on an unsightly wooden telephone pole out front, obstructing a clear view of the building's main facade. Six Amtrak trains still called on the station daily. (Roberta Niesz collection.)

On the night of April 23, 1977, photographer Fred Clark Jr. and friend Tony Lopez undertook an endeavor which managed to successfully capture what was then the character of a downtrodden Tampa Union Station. Lopez dressed as a weary old traveler and, in a visit timed to take place after the last train had departed for the day, was captured in a remarkable series of photographs. Waiting aimlessly and seemingly endlessly, the old man could be found during the next few hours beneath the eaves of the decaying building, lighting a cigarette next to track 5, napping on one of the wooden benches just outside of the building, hunting for change left in the phone booth inside the main waiting room and—in the words of photographer Clark— "looking down the lonely tracks, probably thinking back on better years, better times. . . ." (Fred Clark Jr.)

12

Below and right: Weary traveler Tony Lopez poses under the eaves of a decaying Tampa Union Station, April 23, 1977. (Fred Clark Jr.)

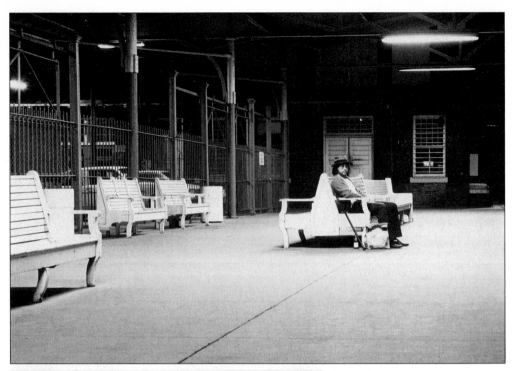

Above and left: Tony Lopez poses here in more photographs at Tampa Union Station, April 23, 1977. (Fred Clark Jr.)

Tony Lopez lights a cigarette while standing next to Tampa Union Station's trademark wrought-iron gates. Fred Clark Jr. recorded this scene at track 5, on the night of April 23, 1977. (Fred Clark Jr.)

As Amtrak tried to revitalize the nation's passenger trains, the changes that Amtrak made to its services, stations, and trains were not always pleasing. Plastic bus station–style seating and painted-steel ashtrays diminished some of the glamour of the waiting room of Tampa Union Station on April 5, 1983. This look had become *de rigeur* in far too many train station waiting rooms in the early years of the Amtrak era. Trim around the edges of the room was largely painted in a color which became known as "Amtrak blue." (Nathan White Jr. photograph, courtesy Barbara Sharkey and Doug Rutledge.)

Tampa Union Station's ticket office had become sadly decrepit by the early 1980s. By then, Amtrak provided the only passenger rail service to the city and the station, and the carrier had merely become a tenant in a crumbling building owned by the corporate descendant of its original owners. Since Amtrak paid no rent, there was no incentive for that descendant—Seaboard System Railroad—to invest maintenance or repair money into the building, and a cash-strapped Amtrak had no such funds, either. Amtrak employees learned to make do, however, and carried on as usual on April 5, 1983. (Nathan White Jr. photograph, courtesy Barbara Sharkey and Doug Rutledge.)

On January 13, 1984, Sims' Crane Service lifted into place a prefabricated structure that would function as Tampa's temporary railroad station for the next 13 1/2 years. The presence of the building was necessitated by Tampa Union Station's continued physical decline. The structure went into place quickly. Although the building was loathed by some (it was derisively called an "Amshack" by a few), it was an effective stop-gap measure and a vast improvement in comfort over Union Station's decrepit waiting room. (Nathan White Jr. photograph, courtesy of Barbara Sharkey and Doug Rutledge.)

Amtrak officials survey progress made in the placement of a temporary ticket office and waiting room at Tampa Union Station, January 13, 1984. Passengers arriving by train for the Super Bowl—held in Tampa that year—found that the 1912 structure which had been Tampa's main railroad terminal for 72 years had been closed to the public. (Nathan White Jr. photograph, courtesy Barbara Sharkey and Doug Rutledge.)

The staircase at the east end of the Tampa Union Station waiting room is shown in this pre-restoration photograph. This staircase once led to the busy offices of the Pullman Company, Tampa Union Station Company, and the railroads which served the station. At the time this picture was taken, though, it had merely become a symbol of a sad decline which bordered on hopeless. (Courtesy of George Cott, Chroma, Inc.)

This pre-restoration photograph of the station's waiting room shows what the ravages of time, deferred maintenance, and 30 years of a leaking roof and skylights had done to the 1912 structure. Scenes like this one brought about feelings of sickness in the hearts of those who

remembered the station's glory days; moreover, they represented a call to action for those who believed the building should be given a new chance for a productive future. (Courtesy of George Cott, Chroma, Inc.)

Water damage from the building's leaky roof was evident everywhere in the structure. This May 1992 photograph shows a water-damaged interior ornament at the northeast corner of the waiting room. (Courtesy of Rowe Architects.)

Abandoned venetian blinds stand eerie sentry at a boarded-up window on the second floor, east wing, of Tampa Union Station. Once someone's office, by May 1992 this space had become filled with fallen plaster and peeling paint, rather than the phone calls and paperwork of workaday railroad life. (Courtesy of Rowe Architects.)

A damaged skylight is open to the sky and the harsh Florida elements in this May 1992 shot. Water poured in through the detached glass pane during each summer thunderstorm from the early 1990s through 1996, further exacerbating the building's physical decline. (Courtesy of Rowe Architects.)

The southeast corner of the station's waiting room suffered from extensive water damage. Deteriorated cornice work, falling plaster, and flaking paint are all too visible in this May 1992 photograph. (Courtesy of Rowe Architects.)

This July 29, 1996 close-up of the cornice work and roof line of the north end of Tampa Union Station reveals that, by that summer, plant growth could be found growing from loose mortar in the masonry of the structure. Happily, a little less than one year later, the building's restoration would be in full swing. (Jackson McQuigg.)

Two
Plant's Empire

Atlantic Coast Line Railroad predecessor Plant System played no small part in the development of Tampa. Company founder H.B. Plant opened the ornate and opulent Tampa Bay Hotel in 1891, but the look of the railroad's steam locomotives was straightforward and simple. Plant System 0-6-0 switcher 122 was built by American Locomotive's Richmond Locomotive Works in 1901, and later became an Atlantic Coast Line locomotive bearing the same number. (American Locomotive Company photograph, Jim Herron collection.)

Shown here is the Tampa Bay Hotel under construction as viewed from the east side of the Hillsborough River sometime between 1888 and 1891. A construction undertaking of this magnitude had never before been attempted in Tampa; in more ways than one, the building project was all about a city striving to reach its potential. Appropriately, the 13 minarets of the

Moorish-architecture hotel have grown to become some of the Tampa's most enduring symbols. This photograph has never before been published. (Courtesy of the Special Collections Department, Merl Kelce Library, University of Tampa.)

In the early years of its existence, certain Plant System passenger trains arrived and departed right from the back doors of the Plant-owned Tampa Bay Hotel, affording hotel guests the ultimate in convenient travel. In 1902, passengers boarded a train at the hotel while well-

wishers politely bid adieu to departing guests from the genteel comfort of one of the hotel's shaded terraces. (Courtesy Tampa-Hillsborough County Public Library.)

This never-before-published photograph was taken in March 1891, one month after the grand opening of Henry Plant's Tampa Bay Hotel. Hotel staff members posed at its main entrance of the new structure, which was designed by J.A. Wood. Judging by the looks of things, these are staff members whose duties kept them outdoors during a normal workday. The mule and stone roller at left was used to compact the stone-topped driveways and walkways around the building in an effort to reduce the amount of dust they generated. (Courtesy of the Special Collections Department, Merl Kelce Library, University of Tampa.)

Three

Heyday

Popular Hollywood actress Lupe Valez arrived at Tampa Union Station on September 17, 1929. She was in town to film a movie at Rocky Point entitled *Hell Harbor*, also starring Jean Hersholt and John Holland, and directed by Henry King. Then, as now, the lives of Hollywood celebrities were points of fascination for average Americans. Tampans had much to talk about in conjunction with Ms. Valez's stay, especially since actor Gary Cooper darkened the doors of Tampa Union Station several times during the course of it. Cooper was in town to visit Ms. Valez during the shooting of the motion picture. (Courtesy Tampa-Hillsborough County Public Library.)

The newly completed Tampa Union Station is seen here on its first day of service—May 15, 1912. The station opened to the traveling public at 6 a.m. that morning. The first stationmaster was Mr. Harry Love; patrons could dine at the lunchroom operated inside the baggage building by Mr. J. Alvarez. "There are also recreation rooms for both sexes, a smoking room for the men, reading rooms, rest rooms, and especial feature is a room furnished with a child's bed, of which women with small children can take advantage," wrote the Tampa *Times* the afternoon before the big day. (Courtesy Tampa-Hillsborough County Public Library.)

A crowd watched a parade honoring World War I draftees being led to Tampa Union Station to leave for duty. Soldiers in "doughboy" uniforms are visible behind the open-topped sedan at the center of the photograph and in the distance on the drive of the station, as they head off to training camps and to fight Europe's sad war of attrition. Some of the young men would see Union Station for the last time, fated to meet their end in the cold and muddy trenches of far-off battlefields, while still others would return, confirmed Tampa members of what would become known as the "Lost Generation." (Courtesy Tampa-Hillsborough County Public Library.)

These two postcard views of the station date from about the time of the station's opening in 1912. In each of the images some artistic license was applied, even to the point of inaccuracy. Architectural ornament which never truly existed—specifically, the ornament bearing an eagle applied to the cornice work at the building's center—even appears on one of the cards. (Courtesy of Special Collections, University of South Florida Library.)

Union Depot, Tampa, Fla.

This is a postcard view of the south elevation of Tampa Union Station. Judging by the horse-and-carriage at the front of the building, this card must have been issued soon after the facility opened in 1912. This tourist postcard—depicting an exaggerated-sized American flag atop the building—was issued by the S.H. Kress & Company 5-and-10¢ store, and was undoubtedly sold at its two stores located near the station, Seventh Avenue in Ybor City and on Florida Avenue downtown, among other places. (Tampa Union Station Preservation & Redevelopment collection.)

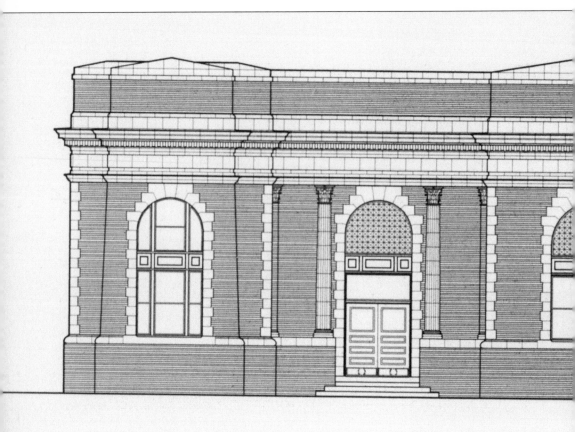

Shown here is an elevation drawing of Tampa Union Station's famous main facade as produced on a computer using a CAD (computer assisted design) program. Revealed are the many details of this Italian Renaissance Revival, brick-and-marble pavilion, including the generous use of columns—which also appeared extensively in architect J.F. Leitner's 1913 Atlantic Coast Line Railroad headquarters building and main passenger station in Wilmington, North Carolina.

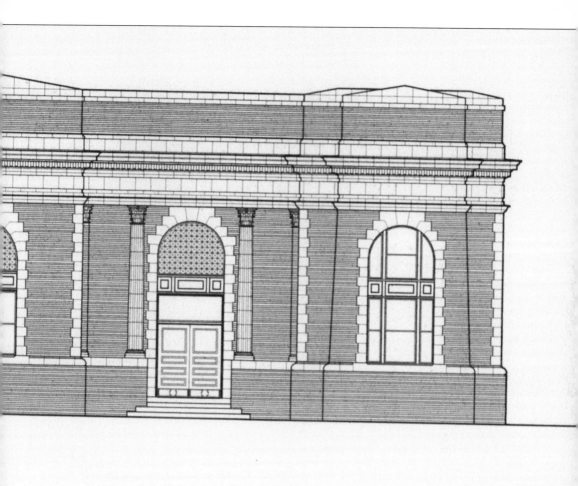

Notable is the presence of the entwined marble "TUS" in an entablature at the center of the building, just above the marble cornice work. This stylized design was used on various elements of the building, including the knobs and brass plates of the station's main doors. (Courtesy of Rowe Architects.)

SCALE IN FEET

These elevations illustrate Building C of the Atlantic Coast Line Railroad headquarters complex in Wilmington, North Carolina. Building C—which contained the railroad's executive office and functioned as the main passenger station for the railroad in Wilmington—was completed in 1913 and designed by architect J.F. Leitner, who designed Tampa Union Station. One doesn't have to look hard to determine similarities between the

two buildings—especially the extensive use of columns and arch motifs on each of the structures. One difference: Tampa Union Station received Corinthian columns, while Building C was decorated with Doric columns. Building C was demolished in 1970, ten years after the railroad relocated its headquarters to Jacksonville, Florida.

Tampa Union Station is barely visible in this 1918 view of the Tampa skyline taken from the west bank of the Hillsborough River. The roof line of the structure is located just to the right of the federal courthouse, another historic Tampa structure that has benefited from a restoration in recent years. The building in the foreground with the lettering on its roof is the Atlantic Coast Line Railroad freight depot, a railroad-operated facility where shipments from local businesses and industries were transshipped onto boxcars or inbound shipments were off-loaded onto delivery trucks. (Courtesy Tampa-Hillsborough County Public Library.)

Some railroad workers posed with the Seaboard Air Line Railway Pacific-type 4-6-2 steam passenger engine 849 at the railroad's division offices at the corner of Whiting and Franklin Streets in downtown Tampa during the 1920s. Engine 849 would proceed to Tampa Union Station to pick up a special train which carried local Shriners to the group's annual convention that year in Kansas City. The locomotive was dressed to the nines for the occasion—and even sported a cartoon of sprinting, fez-wearing Shriners on a board mounted above its headlight. The locomotive was built by the American Locomotive Company's Richmond (Virginia) works in 1913. (M.D. McCarter photograph collection, N11427.)

40

In what is perhaps the most famous photograph of Tampa Union Station, a group of smartly dressed men and women gather on the sidewalk in front of Tampa Union Station alongside Nebraska Avenue on May 15, 1922. The fashions worn by the younger women in the crowd reflect the flapper style which was then becoming popular. This Burgert Brothers photograph resurfaced in local author and historian Hampton Dunn's *Yesterday's Tampa*, published in 1972; the image has come to symbolize the ideals of a preserved Tampa Union Station. (Courtesy Tampa-Hillsborough County Public Library.)

The 1920s scene at the sidewalk in front of Tampa Union Station captured by the Burgert Brothers was later made into a postcard. Thousands of copies of this handsome card were undoubtedly sent back home by vacationers enjoying their stay in "The Cigar City," or at nearby Suncoast beaches. (Courtesy of Seth Bramson, the Bramson Archive.)

41

HOTEL FLORIDAN

Postcards highlighted two of Tampa's finest hotels during the heyday of Tampa Union Station. The Hotel Floridan on Florida Avenue opened on January 15, 1927. It featured the popular Sapphire Room, one of Tampa's leading nightclubs until well after World War II. Hotel guests through the years included the Cincinnati Reds baseball team, which came to Tampa each year to participate in spring training at Al Lopez Field, and actor Charlton Heston; all passed through Tampa Union Station. Another one of Tampa's finest hotels then was the Mirasol Hotel, on Davis Islands (below). Happily, both of these Tampa landmarks have become focal points of historic preservation projects: the Mirasol has been restored and the Floridan's rejuvenation is planned. (Florida State Archives.)

"It has been decided by the Union Station Company to make a beautiful park in front of the station, where there is an acre of ground. . . .," gushed the Tampa *Times* on May 14, 1912, the day before the station opened. Indeed, the princely sum of $6,000 had been set aside to create the park—a considerable amount, considering the cost of the station was $250,000 in its entirety. On October 11, 1921, a caretaker worked on the park land in front of the station, the appearance of which was marred by the boastful billboard erected by a well-meaning board of trade. The oak tree—which predated the station—has since passed on. (Courtesy Tampa-Hillsborough County Public Library.)

Long before slogans such as Tampa: "Where the Good Life Gets Better Every Day" and "Tampa: America's Next Great City," there were others, including this one, "Florida's Year 'Round City." This sign was placed prominently on the Tampa Union Station lawn and parallel to Nebraska Avenue when this picture was taken on October 11, 1921. For information regarding the city's restroom facilities, one merely had to call at the Information Bureau operated by the Board of Trade, on the first floor of City Hall. (Courtesy Tampa-Hillsborough County Public Library.)

On May 1, 1937, Yellow Cab drivers posed in front of the station after winning a special award for driving without a single accident in 1936. Visible behind them is another fact of life in what was then the Jim Crow South: hand-painted lettering on a window indicates that the doors on the south side of the station led to a waiting room for whites only, where social protocol and state laws dictated black men and women dare not tread. For purposes of segregation, the station was split down the middle into two stations, with a black waiting room on the north side of the building and a white waiting room on the south. (Courtesy Tampa-Hillsborough County Public Library.)

Through the years, Tampa Union Station found itself being used as a backdrop for thousands of photographs. But not all of them depicted celebrities or mom and the kids ready to depart on the northbound *Southern States Special*. On May 1, 1937, five Yellow Cab drivers posed in front of the station after winning a special award from Globe Indemnity Co. honoring their respective lack of accidents for three consecutive years—1934, 1935, and 1936. (Courtesy Tampa-Hillsborough County Public Library.)

Atlantic Coast Line Railroad 467 is a classic example of a steam locomotive used by the Coast Line on passenger trains from the 1920s through the 1940s. Pictured here at the railroad's UCETA yards just east of the city, 467 was of the 4-6-2 wheel arrangement (four leading wheels, six driving wheels, and two trailing wheels), thereby classifying it as a Pacific-type locomotive. It was built by the Baldwin Locomotive Works of Philadelphia, Pennsylvania. (Courtesy Tampa-Hillsborough County Public Library.)

On May 10, 1924, the Union Transfer Company posed its nine trucks, drivers, laborers, and managers in front of the express and baggage buildings at the station's south side. Union Transfer Company was the local affiliate of American Railway Express, the firm then responsible for handling many time-critical express rail shipments. By 1929, American Railway Express would be replaced by the Railway Express Agency, which was jointly owned by the railroad companies. American Railway Express was left to focus on other aspects of its operations, including its fledgling financial services business. Ultimately American Railway Express would have the last laugh; its revised identity with a slightly shortened name—American Express—is recognized the world over. (Courtesy Tampa-Hillsborough County Public Library.)

Tampa Electric Company operated a fleet of streetcars that lasted in the city until 1946. Here is car 156 at the trolley barn it called home, on March 26, 1930. The roller sign highlights the route to which 156 was assigned that day, namely the run between Tampa Union Station and another railroad destination: Gary, home of the Tampa Northern Railroad's repair shops. The Tampa Northern was acquired by the Seaboard Air Line Railway in 1912, although it was operated as a separate subsidiary of the bigger line until the 1920s. The Seaboard kept the Gary Shops open well into the 1960s. (Courtesy Tampa-Hillsborough County Public Library.)

Europe was at war, but that didn't stop Tampa citizens from having a good time during the city's annual Gasparilla celebration and parade on a bright Monday afternoon in February 1941. That year, the parade for the annual city holiday—which pays homage to mythical pirate Jose Gaspar—played host to a float entered by the Seaboard Air Line Railway. The float—which promoted the *Orange Blossom Special* and *Silver Meteor*, trains which served Tampa Union Station—featured decorative images of diesel-electric locomotives like those that pulled these fine Northeast-Florida speedsters. (Courtesy Tampa-Hillsborough County Public Library.)

For purposes of this book, the focal point of this April 29, 1926 photograph by Burgert Brothers, Commercial Photographers, is at the extreme right. This is Zack Street and the newly completed Atlantic Ice and Coal Company facility; Tampa Union Station peers out of and into the picture at the end of the thoroughfare. Atlantic's building has an interesting story of its own. Converted to professional offices after the firm moved out, the building still stands, although it is currently vacant. (Courtesy Tampa-Hillsborough County Public Library.)

All appears calm and routine in this scene as the Atlantic Coast Line's *Tampa Special* prepares to depart from Tampa Union Station's track 1 in 1922. (Courtesy Tampa-Hillsborough County Public Library.)

7295

There is one in every crowd. Just as the conductor of Coast Line's *Tampa Special* strikes a dignified pose with the trains flagman next to the end of his train, one of the passengers on the platform of the observation car takes notice and hams it up for the camera with an animated

48

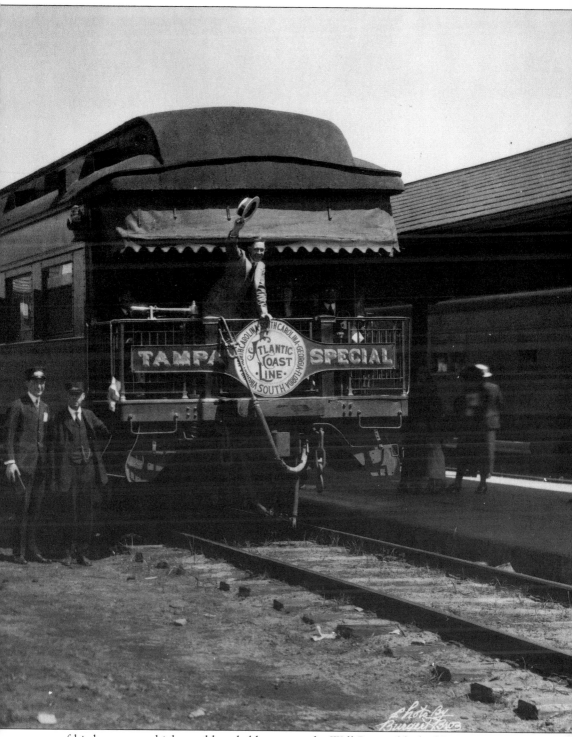

wave of his hat—one which would probably even make Will Rogers blush. (Courtesy Tampa Hillsborough County Public Library.)

"All tickets!" Who could forget this familiar refrain of railroad conductors everywhere? Aboard a coach occupied by a group of very dignified-looking passengers, an Atlantic Coast Line conductor punches tickets on a Coast Line passenger train during the 1940s. (Barringer Studio.)

Pictured here is 4-6-2 Pacific-type steam locomotive 424 on an Atlantic Coast Line passenger train at Tampa Union Station during the 1950s. The great number of cars for express on this train suggests that it was one of the railroad's secondary runs. Diesel-electric locomotive 648 is shifting other Coast Line passenger equipment on an adjacent track. (William J. Lenoir photograph, Jim Herron collection.)

Burgert Brothers, Commercial Photographers, captured the scene as a group of largely African-American men left their families behind to board a special train for an Emergency Relief Council forest camp, June 5, 1933. The expressions worn by the faces are revealing:

some are frightened, others hopeful; all are anxious. (Courtesy Tampa-Hillsborough County Public Library.)

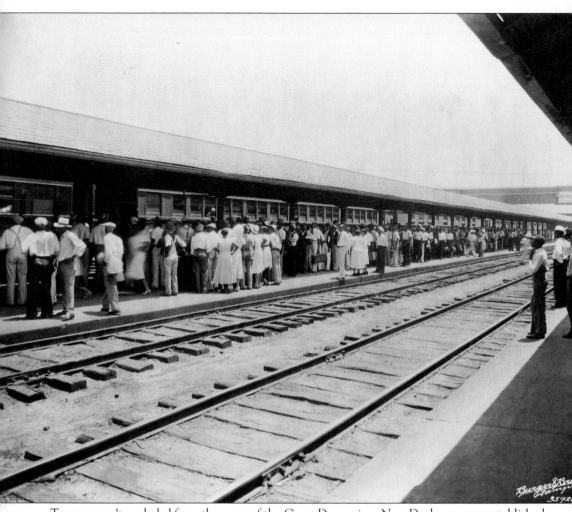

Tampa wasn't excluded from the woes of the Great Depression. New Deal programs established by President Franklin Roosevelt provided a much-needed boost to the nation's ailing economy. It was with this "rising-tide-lifts-all-boats mentality" that the federal Emergency Relief Council operated several forest camps in the Southeast. On June 5, 1933, a large group of Tampans left the station for one of these camps, hoping to find prosperity—or at least survival—there. (Courtesy Tampa-Hillsborough County Public Library.)

Four
After the War

The Hillsboro News Company issued more than one postcard of Tampa Union Station for sale at local newsstands. Commercial postcards produced following World War II, such as this one from the late 1940s, tended to emphasize the beautiful landscaping of the depot's front lawn, rather than the building itself, sadly contributing to its postwar decline. Perceptions of the station were beginning to change; the structure no longer represented modernity, as it once had. (Author's collection.)

An Atlantic Coast Line Railway Post Office (RPO) car is pictured at the station January 18, 1949. Cars like this one operated until the 1960s. Mail was sorted en route on RPOs. Eventually the post office found the savings achieved by moving mail by truck or plane outweighed the additional burden of having to sort the mail before it was transported. The statistics are disheartening: 2,600 RPOs were in service in 1956; 1,400 remained by 1961; 741 were in service by 1967; and, by 1977, just 2 RPOs remained. Today there aren't any RPOs in service, although Amtrak does transport a great deal of pre-sorted mail on its trains. (Courtesy Tampa-Hillsborough County Public Library.)

Purple-gold-and-silver E6-model diesel-electric locomotives on an Atlantic Coast Line passenger train at Tampa Union Station were captured on film during the late 1940s. The passenger train is being switched after heading into the station's track 1 upon arrival from colder climes to the north. (William J. Lenoir photograph, Jim Herron collection.)

Seaboard Air Line E4 locomotive 3010 and two other locomotives pulled the *Palmland* through Savannah, Georgia, on July 4, 1948. The Northeast-Florida *Palmland*—with through service to Tampa and Miami from New York, Hartford, and Boston—is a good example of one of the Seaboard's secondary trains, which stopped at many of the smaller towns the Seaboard served or, as some big-city-types chose to derisively put it, "at every little pig path along the way." (R.D. Sharpless photograph, F.E. Ardrey Jr. collection.)

The Seaboard Air Line Railroad's *Silver Meteor* was photographed at Savannah, Georgia, on July 4, 1948. E7 diesel-electric locomotive 3028 and two other units have both the Tampa/St. Petersburg and Miami sections of the train comfortably in tow. At Wildwood, in the center of the Sunshine State, the two sections of the train would be split and independently sent on to their respective east and west coast Florida destinations. (R.D. Sharpless photograph, F.E. Ardrey Jr. collection.)

Seaboard also entered a float in the 1954 Gasparilla festivities. Here, during that year's Gasparilla night parade, Seaboard's float passes by the old J.J. Newberry variety store at the intersection of Cass Street and Franklin Street. Although Seaboard that year chose a pirate ship theme for its float instead of railroading, its participation in the parade represented just another way for the railroad to keep its name in front of travelers and shippers alike. And even without a decorative *Orange Blossom Special* astride it, the railroad's float still proudly rivaled those from other entrants, such as the Maas Brothers department store chain. (Courtesy Tampa-Hillsborough County Public Library.)

A photograph taken of the station by Burgert Brothers, Commercial Photographers, on October 15, 1952, was transformed into this postcard. The colortone card—published by Tampa's Hillsboro News Company—managed to make Tampa Union Station's front lawn look just a bit greener and the colors of the hibiscus a little bit brighter than they were in real life. Wonder how many of these cards were sold in the station's newsstand in a given year? (Author's collection.)

The station appears to be aging gracefully in this October 15, 1952 photograph. Rainwater has streaked the marble at the cornice work of the building, giving an appropriate and dignified stain of time to the proud facility. A Yellow Cab waits patiently under the port-cochere for a fare from an incoming Atlantic Coast Line or Seaboard Air Line train. (Courtesy Tampa-Hillsborough County Public Library.)

Here is Tampa Union Station as it appeared in the 1960s. Tracks used by the Seaboard Air Line are at left, while those used by the Atlantic Coast Line are at right. On the far right sits the Coast Line's main line to Port Tampa, while a sign at the east end of the yard reminds passers-by that the station grounds are property of Tampa Union Station Company, which was jointly owned by the two railroads. (William J. Lenoir photograph, Atlantic Coast Line and Seaboard Air Line Railroads Historical Society collection.)

Both the Atlantic Coast Line Railroad and competitor Seaboard Air Line Railroad used freight cars in their fleet as rolling billboards advertising their crack passenger trains. Seaboard boxcar 19361 was painted in a scheme plugging travel on the *Silver Meteor* when photographed at Tampa in the 1950s. (William J. Lenoir photograph, Jim Herron collection.)

The naming of railroad passenger cars was a time-honored railroad practice, and it assisted railroad personnel in readily identifying the configuration of passenger cars without being forced to resort to an equipment roster. Large capacity twin-unit dining car "Port Tampa" was no exception. The diner and its sister kitchen car were photographed at the coach yards at Tampa's UCETA Yard during the 1950s. (William J. Lenoir photograph, Jim Herron collection.)

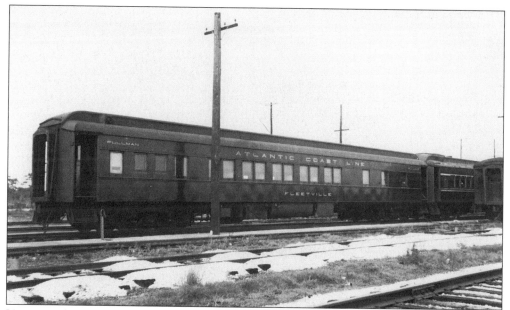

Here is Atlantic Coast Line Pullman sleeping car "Fleetville" at the railroad's coach yard at Tampa's UCETA Yard during the 1950s. Incredibly, some 1920s-vintage sleeping cars like this one remained in service on American railroads until well into the 1960s. (William J. Lenoir photograph, Jim Herron collection.)

In this railroad publicity photograph, female passengers visit for a moment aboard the women's salon of a coach on a streamlined passenger train, c. 1950. (Courtesy of the Atlanta History Center.)

Atlantic Coast Line locomotive 511 had just delivered one of the railroad's streamliners to Tampa Union Station during the 1950s. The large overhead canopy shown sitting astride track 2 was demolished in 1988. (William J. Lenoir photograph, Jim Herron collection.)

Diesel-electric locomotive 531 headed an Atlantic Coast Line passenger train into Tampa Union Station during the 1950s. The train—which is perhaps the *West Coast Champion*—consisted of six passenger cars that day, including a combination coach-baggage car. (William J. Lenoir photograph, Jim Herron collection.)

A rounded-end observation lounge car often punctuated a streamlined passenger train. These teardrop-shaped passenger cars—which featured unparalleled views of scenery going by—were frequent sights on trains at Tampa Union Station. In a c. 1950 photograph, a group of pleasant-looking passengers seems to be quite at home aboard one such car. (Courtesy of the Atlanta History Center.)

A Seaboard Air Line Railroad baggage car is shown at the express building at Tampa Union Station during the 1950s. Parcels and packages for both the Post Office Department and REA Express, the successor to the Railway Express Agency, came through this facility on a daily basis. Sadly, it is one part of the station which is gone forever. The building was demolished during the 1980s. (William J. Lenoir photograph, Jim Herron collection.)

The competition looms in this photograph. Not coincidentally, the number of passenger trains serving Tampa Union Station declined as airports and air service improved. The numbers are staggering. From 34 passenger trains per day through Tampa in 1938, the numbers had declined to 28 by 1959, and to just 6 by the time the present Tampa International Airport opened in 1971. In a February 27, 1939 photograph, the WPA-constructed terminal building at Peter O' Knight Airport on Davis Islands in Tampa is shown; National Airlines and Eastern Airlines then served what was the city's principal commercial airport, largely with DC-2 and DC-3 aircraft. (Courtesy Tampa-Hillsborough County Public Library.)

Things would change quickly, and a November 20, 1952 photograph illustrates just how much. A National Airlines DC-4 sits on the ramp at the postwar Tampa International Airport, built on the site of a former private airstrip-turned-World War II air base, Drew Field. The newer facility boasted a dining room, cocktail lounge, and service from carriers with names—such as Trans-Canada Air Lines—which would have had an exotic ring to airline passengers of just a generation before. (Courtesy Tampa-Hillsborough County Public Library.)

A group of fresh U.S. Navy recruits posed with their NCO escort for a group portrait under Tampa Union Station's eaves during the 1950s. The young men were headed to training camp, and ultimately the assignments, bases, and ships of the Korean Conflict, a war thousands of miles away from the station's front door. (Courtesy of Hampton Dunn Collection, Special Collections, University of South Florida Library.)

Parting shot. As his family looks on, a young U.S. Navy recruit kisses his girl good-bye before departing for training camp with other Navy draftees from the Tampa area; this scene took place at the station in the midst of the Korean Conflict. Young soldiers and sailors left Tampa from Union Station to serve in World War I, World War II, Korea, and Vietnam. For some, it was the last sight of home they ever experienced. (Courtesy of Hampton Dunn Collection, Special Collections, University of South Florida Library.)

Coaches belonging to the Atlantic Coast Line were photographed at the railroad's UCETA Yard during the 1950s. Passenger equipment from Coast Line trains terminating at Tampa Union Station was stored at the facility when idle; the railroad also maintained a repair facility for passenger cars at the site. (William J. Lenoir photograph, Jim Herron collection.)

Shown here is an African-American locomotive fireman aboard a diesel-electric locomotive during the 1950s. African-Americans on locomotive crews in the South were afflicted with a particular plight. Agreements between white labor unions and the railroads effectively barred them from being promoted to locomotive engineers, the natural course of promotion for white members of locomotive crews. With the advent of the diesel-electric locomotive, the role of locomotive firemen hung precariously in the balance. Black railroaders were not given the chance to become full-fledged locomotive engineers until the Civil Rights Movement of the 1960s. (Courtesy of the Atlanta History Center.)

A group of businessmen enjoy dinner aboard a dining car on a streamliner in this railroad publicity photograph from the 1950s. Wonder if the tomatoes served aboard were just a bit smaller on everyday runs? (Courtesy of the Atlanta History Center.)

This scene at the express building at Tampa Union Station was taken during the 1950s. The Railway Express Agency had by then been renamed REA Express. Still owned by the nation's railroads, the organization's name was changed to reflect the fact that rail was no longer its only method of transporting express. By the 1950s, in fact, a goodly percentage of Railway Express Agency packages were moving in the cargo holds of commercial airliners. (William J. Lenoir photograph, Jim Herron collection.)

Southern Railway never served Tampa Union Station, but this famous 1950 publicity picture from that railroad speaks for all of the couples who boarded a Pullman sleeping car for points north at stations throughout the Southeast. One can almost feel the anticipation of the trip which lay ahead. Which do you suppose would be most exciting? The destination or the getting there? (Courtesy of the Atlanta History Center.)

A northbound Atlantic Coast Line passenger train at Ybor City is shown here during the early 1950s. Judging by the number of passenger cars on this streamliner, it is the peak of Florida's winter season. Just minutes before, scores of vacationers had boarded the train at Tampa Union Station, ready to return to the Northeast and home aboard passenger equipment operated by "The Standard Railroad of the South." (William J. Lenoir photograph, Jim Herron collection.)

A Railway Express Agency-lettered express reefer car was photographed in the vicinity of Tampa Union Station during the 1950s. Cars like this one were operated at the head-end of regularly-scheduled passenger trains, speeding winter fruit and vegetables and other perishables from the Sunshine State to points north. (William J. Lenoir photograph, Jim Herron collection.)

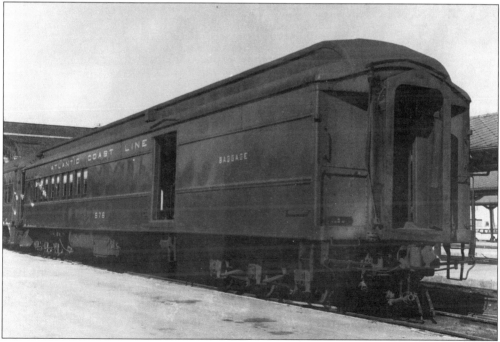

An old Atlantic Coast Line combination car is pictured at Tampa Union Station in the mid-1960s. These cars were so named because they served a number of functions, with interior configurations to match. Car 676, pictured here, contained both a coach section and a baggage section. (Jim Herron.)

A dining car crew posed for a photograph aboard a lunch-counter car in a passenger train of the mid-1950s. (Courtesy of the Atlanta History Center.)

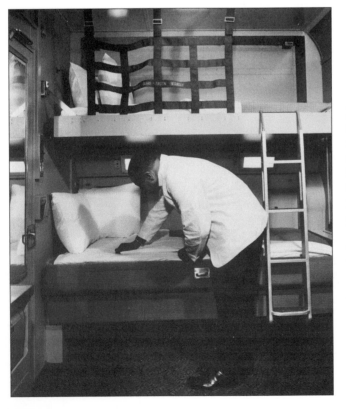

Here, a Pullman porter makes up a sleeping car berth in a bedroom on a streamlined train *c.* 1950. In just slightly over a decade from the time this photograph was made, A. Philip Randolph, the leader of the Brotherhood of Sleeping Car Porters, would crystallize his place in history thanks to his introduction of Martin Luther King Jr.'s "I have a dream" speech at the 1963 March on Washington, and his ardent participation in the successful efforts to pass the Civil Rights Act of 1964. (Courtesy of the Atlanta History Center.)

The west coast section of the Seaboard Air Line Railroad's *Silver Meteor* was photographed at Tampa on November 25, 1966. E7-model diesel-electric locomotive 3045—delivered to the Seaboard by the Electro-Motive Division of General Motors in April 1949—is in charge of the train, one which was no doubt filled with early-winter-season vacationers and tourists. (William J. Husa Jr. photograph, Joseph L. Oates collection.)

The caption on this early-1960s postcard reads as follows: "The *Silver Meteor*, Seaboard Air Line Railroad's popular all-reserved coach and Pullman streamliner, in service throughout the year between New York and both coasts of Florida." And what could make a postcard scene more Florida-like than oranges still on the tree? Reportedly, railroad photographers brought with them a tree limb, replete with ripe oranges, to the photograph shoot. The tree branch was, of course, deliberately held in the frame to create this appealing orange grove shot. (Author's collection.)

Passengers enjoy themselves aboard a lounge car on a streamlined passenger train *c.* 1950. The bartender is busy with chores, while the well-dressed young man on the right is busily chatting with the woman sitting next to him; from the looks of things, she's far more interested in the scenery going by the train as it speeds towards its destination. (Courtesy of the Atlanta History Center.)

Seaboard Air Line Railroad diesel-electric locomotive 2702 is shown at Tampa Union Station during the 1950s. The locomotive, built by Baldwin-Lima-Hamilton of Lima, Ohio, is a DR6-4-15 model, one of only nine of the type constructed by the manufacturer. Nicknamed "Babyface" Baldwins by railroad crews for obvious reasons, Seaboard at times used them on the railroad's Tampa-Venice and Tampa-Port Boca Grande connections to and from the *Silver Meteor.* (Howard Robins photograph, Jim Herron collection.)

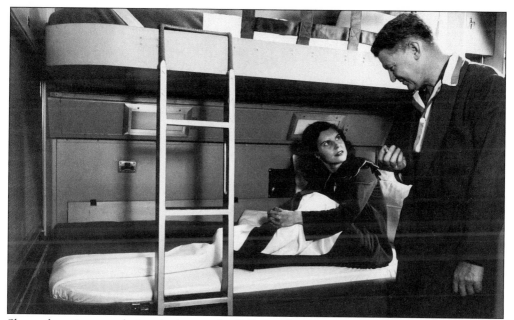

Shown here is a couple in a bedroom of a Pullman sleeping car, *c.* 1950. In a room with this particular configuration, during nighttime the top bunk was unlatched and folded out from the wall. The bottom bunk was revealed by folding down the sofa, which provided daytime seating accommodations. Rooms like this one also contained private restroom facilities. (Courtesy of the Atlanta History Center.)

Atlantic Coast Line's *West Coast Champion* was photographed at Tampa Union Station on August 9, 1966. Diesel locomotive 539 and its train have headed into the station and are shown on track 1. The train's consist is swollen due to a nationwide airlines strike which took place during July and August of that year; thanks to the strike, trains were—for a time, at least—again the nation's primary means of commercial transport. (C.L. Goolsby.)

The Tampa section of Seaboard Air Line Railroad's *Silver Meteor* backed into Tampa Union Station under the shadow of the landmark Peoples Gas System storage tank on August 8, 1966. The nationwide airlines strike which ran the course of July and August of that year caused Seaboard and competitor Coast Line to run unusually large trains in a month which ordinarily fell in the middle of Florida's off-season. (C.L. Goolsby.)

In this scene at Tampa Union Station, August 9, 1966, Atlantic Coast Line Railroad locomotive 537 is switching a combination car from one track to another, while a smaller switch engine is performing similar duties on a track at left. Cars from the Pennsylvania Railroad and the Central of Georgia Railway are on a track on 537's right; the foreign cars are probably on the *West Coast Champion*. (C.L. Goolsby.)

74

A set of Atlantic Coast Line Railroad diesel-electric locomotives cleared the switch located just across Nebraska Avenue from Tampa Union Station on August 9, 1966. The buildings to the immediate left of the locomotives have led a varied existence through the years. Their identities and ownerships have changed numerous times through the years—Alberta Hotel, Union Station Hotel and Bath, and the Arcade Bar—but the buildings, although derelict, still stand as of this writing. (C.L. Goolsby.)

Once in a while even freight cars could be found on Tampa Union Station's tracks. Shortly after the merger which created the Seaboard Coast Line in 1967, the railroad fielded a celebratory display train at the station, displaying experimental high-capacity hopper car 500000 (known as the "Whopper Hopper"), among other pieces of freight equipment and a locomotive. (Jim Herron collection.)

The June 1967 merger of the Atlantic Coast Line and Seaboard Air Line railroads created a new carrier—called Seaboard Coast Line Railroad. W.T. Rice, president of Seaboard Coast Line, issued orders requiring all locomotives in the railroad's fleet to be quickly re-lettered with the name of the new company. The result was the hasty application of new markings over existing paint schemes. Locomotive 593—in Seaboard Coast Line lettering but still bearing Seaboard Air Line–applied mint green paint and orange accent stripes—presents a perfect example of this directive at Tampa Union Station in 1967. (Jim Herron collection.)

Even as the Tampa skyline continued to evolve and change, Tampa Union Station remained a busy place in March 1965. Two trains apiece of the Atlantic Coast Line Railroad and rival Seaboard Air Line Railroad are in evidence on the station's tracks, while a number of Alco, Baldwin, and Electro-Motive Division diesel-electric switchers stand-by, ready to shift cars on the station house tracks and to nearby coach yards. (Emery J. Gulash photograph, Joseph L. Oates collection.)

At Tampa Union Station—or, more specifically at Nebraska Avenue and near the present location of Nick Nuccio Parkway—once stood a watchman's tower. The purpose of the watchman stationed inside was to protect trains and motorists at the railroad street crossing located beside it. In this late 1960s view, both railroad and tower are showing wear-and-tear from both many years of faithful service and too much deferred maintenance. (William J. Lenoir photograph, Jim Herron collection.)

Here, Seaboard Coast Line Railroad train 258, the Tampa-Venice connection to the railroad's *Silver Meteor*, departs Tampa Union Station for Venice in May 1968. "Doodlebug" locomotive 4900—nicknamed as such because the distinguished-looking combination locomotive-baggage car resembled the self-propelled "Doodlebug" passenger cars of other railroads—was built by the St. Louis Car Company in 1936. It boasted 600 horsepower. (Jim Herron.)

From time to time mishaps did occur, even in the "good old days." On August 6, 1968, a large derrick worked to clear the wreck of a Seaboard Coast Line passenger train at Winter Haven, Florida, near Cypress Gardens. On this run, passengers wishing to see a Florida orange grove up close for the first time must have felt like they got just a bit more than they bargained for! (Ken Ardinger photograph, F.E. Ardrey Jr. collection.)

At a time when other railroads were saddled with sagging ridership numbers and decrepit passenger equipment, Seaboard Coast Line passenger trains continued to thrive. Indeed, company president W.T. Rice and his management team remained optimistic about the future of the passenger train, and continued to view the operation of quality passenger service as unsurpassable advertising for the road's freight service. Popular Florida destinations and stylish advertising typified by the railroad's December 11, 1970 timetable showed an energetic Seaboard Coast Line keeping pace with a quickly changing society that had recently put man onto the moon. (Author's collection.)

Seaboard Coast Line Railroad locomotive 579, an E8 model built by the Electro-Motive Division of General Motors, at Tampa Union Station with the Tampa–Sarasota–Fort Myers connection to the railroad's *West Coast Champion* appears here in an August 4, 1970 photograph. (Jim Herron.)

Seaboard Coast Line's December 11, 1970 timetable featured artwork of a New York–Florida streamliner heading into a brilliant sunburst. (Author's collection.)

During the late 1960s and early 1970s, the Railway Express Agency struggled for its life. From 1929 until the 1950s, the firm was virtually unchallenged in its role as the principal carrier of time-critical packages and parcels. Competition from firms such as United Parcel Service—once, ironically enough, a Railway Express Agency affiliate—would ultimately spell the demise of the company. On August 25, 1970, truck 5A924 was at the express building at Tampa Union Station, bearing the final logo and livery used by the Railway Express Agency before it folded in the mid-1970s. (Joseph L. Oates.)

Passengers gather their bags to board a Seaboard Coast Line passenger train at Tampa Union Station, 1967. The car at the rear of this train is known as a "blunt-end" observation lounge. When at the rear of a train, large windows at the end of such cars afforded passengers scenic views and a vista of receding railroad track. However—and unlike rounded-end observation cars with designs which obligated their operation to the rear of any given train— blunt-end cars were flexible, capable of being operated anywhere within a train's consist. (Jim Herron.)

Amtrak's *Silver Star* is pictured at Tampa Union Station in June 1971. Judging by outward appearances, not much had changed since Amtrak's takeover of Seaboard Coast Line passenger trains on May 1 of that year. Diesel-electric locomotive 535 was manufactured for Seaboard Coast Line-predecessor Atlantic Coast Line by the Electro-Motive Division of General Motors. (Jim Herron.)

The west coast section of Amtrak's *South Wind* is shown nearing Tampa Union Station on May 20, 1971. Broadway Avenue is just out of sight at left from the photographer's vantage point in this picture, and the long-gone Ralston Purina feed mill near the old Spanish Park restaurant is barely visible in the distance. Amtrak was but 20 days old when this photograph was taken of locomotive 594 and its one sleeping car, one coach train. On this day, the train was likely running late as it is heading in—rather than backing in—to the station. (F.E. Ardrey Jr. collection.)

The St. Petersburg/Clearwater/Tampa and Miami-Chicago Amtrak *South Wind* (later the *Floridian*) was a political football from the time of Amtrak's inception in 1971. Problems with poor track conditions led to several derailments and re-routings, and ultimately a slow, 36-hour, Florida-to-Chicago schedule; these troubles led to low ridership. The train's plight was commented upon by writer Lewis Grizzard in his book *Kathy Sue Loudermilk, I Love You*, in 1979; Grizzard argued the train should be given a fighting chance, but sadly, it was discontinued that same year. The two-car St. Petersburg/Tampa section of the train is at Tampa Union Station on September 24, 1972, in the safe charge of former Seaboard Coast Line E8 diesel-electric locomotive 554. (Fred Clark Jr.)

Amtrak was created on May 1, 1971, the result of the creation by Congress of the National Railroad Passenger Corporation. Passenger services of 20 member railroads—including the Seaboard Coast Line—were taken over by the quasi-governmental Amtrak, and by the summer of 1971 equipment from the various member railroads was re-shuffled throughout the country to where it was thought it was needed most. Some pieces of railroad rolling stock wound up far from their original homes, such as former Illinois Central E9-model locomotive 4034, shown at Tampa Union Station on November 11, 1972. (S.H. Jackowski photograph, Jim Herron collection.)

Private railroad car "Florida Surf" is pictured on the rear of Amtrak's *Champion* at Tampa Union Station, 1972. A former Pullman sleeping car, the "Florida Surf" was built by the Pullman-Standard Car Manufacturing Company for the Louisville & Nashville Railroad. It was later sold to a private individual and Tampa resident in 1971. When pictured, the car was on the outbound leg of a Tampa-Jacksonville round-trip charter run. Note the "TUS" planter still sitting next to the button-block at track 3. (Jim Herron.)

Former Union Pacific Railroad E9 locomotive 954 showed up at Tampa Union Station on January 26, 1973, thanks to Amtrak's creation of a national pool of railroad passenger equipment from the fleets of its 20-member railroads. The 954 was built in the 1950s for the Omaha-based Union Pacific. Accustomed to seeing service on trains of its former parent, such as the *City of Denver* or the *City of Los Angeles*, in its third decade the 954 found itself becoming familiar with routes emanating from Florida instead. (August Staebler photograph, Jim Herron collection.)

In April 1974, Amtrak was still operating scores of cars and locomotives in the paint and lettering schemes of their previous owners. Many of Amtrak's locomotives and all of its passenger cars in those early days dated from the 1940s and 1950s. A case in point is former Seaboard Coast Line Railroad diesel-electric locomotive 5557, an E7 model originally manufactured for the Atlantic Coast Line Railroad by the Electro-Motive Division of General Motors. (Jim Herron.)

Seaboard Coast Line (and later, successors Seaboard System Railroad and CSX Transportation) didn't entirely give up all of its passenger equipment with the advent of Amtrak in 1971. Railroad office cars utilized by company executives were one notable example, such as Seaboard Coast Line office car 306, shown at Tampa Union Station on January 27, 1975. Since these cars routinely traveled on the back of regularly scheduled Amtrak trains, for a time Amtrak-style red-white-and-blue striping was commonplace on cars like 306, and in 1975 it was no exception. This practice—intended to afford Amtrak passenger trains a more or less consistent look at all times—had generally ended by the early 1980s. (August Staebler photograph, Jim Herron collection.)

The southbound Amtrak *Champion* was photographed at Tampa Union Station on September 4, 1977. Here, the Florida–New York train backs across the railroad grade crossing at Nebraska Avenue so it can switch tracks—from the former Seaboard Air Line to the former Atlantic Coast Line—after arriving from St. Petersburg and Clearwater. (Fred Clark Jr.)

In this mid-1970s view, two women visit in a sleeping car bedroom aboard a passenger train. Though the Pullman Company was long gone by this time, passengers could still enjoy rooms aboard former Pullman sleeping cars on Amtrak and a few remaining privately operated passenger trains in North America. (Courtesy of the Atlanta History Center.)

Hungry, anyone? Railroad passengers of many generations fondly recall past train trips by the quality of the food in the dining car. A large dining car steak dinner with all the trimmings like this one was certain to be a happy precursor to a fun night of socializing with fellow passengers in the train's lounge car. (Courtesy of the Atlanta History Center.)

Perhaps happily dreaming about his forthcoming visit to Grandma's, a young boy takes a nap aboard a coach of a passenger train during the mid-1970s. (Courtesy of the Atlanta History Center.)

On April 7, 1979, Tampa Union Station became a movie set. A steam locomotive—former Reader Railroad 2-6-2 number 11—and a set of steam-era passenger cars were brought in for the filming of the movie *Golden Honeymoon*, starring James Whitmore and Teresa Wright. One of the platforms at the station—for a moment in Hollywood time—took on the appearance of another locale: a train station in Trenton, New Jersey. (Fred Clark Jr.)

Here, a fellow actor talks to actor James Whitmore during a break in the filming of the major motion picture *Golden Honeymoon* at Tampa Union Station, April 7, 1979. (Jim Herron.)

It is dusk on January 30, 1979, as the southbound Amtrak *Champion*, headed to its final two destinations—Clearwater and St. Petersburg—rushes by the northbound Amtrak *Floridian*, which is patiently waiting on a siding. The *Floridian* is headed towards Tampa Union Station

and Nashville, Louisville, Indianapolis, and other stops along the way to its final destination of Chicago, while the *Champion* is nearing the end of its run from the frigid Northeast to the land of palm trees and sunshine. (Fred Clark Jr.)

A member of the locomotive crew descends the steps from the cab of locomotive 545 on Amtrak's Northeast-Florida *Champion* at Tampa Union Station, May 1974. The clock tower of City Hall is clearly visible at right in this photograph, while Tampa Union Station's now-demolished express building and several highway trucks of Railway Express Agency descendant REA Express are in the left portion of the picture. (Jim Herron.)

"I'm Donna. Fly me to New York." In the 1970s, with catch-phrases such as this one, National Airlines ran a well-known series of advertisements in which the company invited the traveling public to fly its jets—each of which had been given a feminine name—to cities on its route map. The campaign was too much for a group of Tampa Bay area railroad enthusiasts, who, with the complicity of an Amtrak employee or two, styled locomotive 242 into "Melvin," which invited crews to run "him" to Chicago. The engine is seen here departing Tampa Union Station with Amtrak's Florida-Chicago *Floridian* in January 1974. (Jim Herron.)

Shown here are Amtrak locomotives 607 and 605 on the *Champion* at Tampa Union Station, August 1974. The SDP40F-model diesel-electric locomotives were then brand-new, having been built by the Electro-Motive Division of General Motors in 1973–1974, and were rated at 3,000 horsepower apiece. Part of the downtown Tampa skyline—including the First Financial Tower, General Telephone building, and Exchange Bank building (left to right)—is visible behind the train. (Jim Herron.)

Amtrak train 92, the *Champion*, arrived at Tampa Union Station from St. Petersburg and Clearwater in September 1974 with SDP40F-model locomotive 611 on the point. Stops to be made on the *Champion*'s northward Florida–New York trek included Jacksonville, Savannah, Charleston, Washington D.C., Baltimore, and Philadelphia. (Jim Herron.)

Prior to the 1982 start of the original Tampa-Miami *Silver Palm*, Amtrak and Seaboard Coast Line operated a test train over the train's proposed route. Here, the test train—with a mostly-Amtrak consist save for Seaboard Coast Line business car 309 on the rear—backs past Nick Nuccio Parkway into Tampa Union Station. (Joseph L. Oates.)

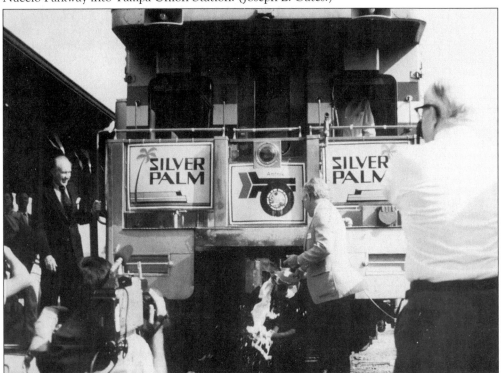

A bottle of champagne is broken over the rear coupler of Amtrak office car 10000 by an official to celebrate the debut of a new train, the Tampa-Miami *Silver Palm*. The train—a collaboration between Amtrak and the Florida Department of Transportation—was operated from November 1982 until February 1985, although Amtrak has since recycled the name of the train for another *Silver Palm*. Standing next to car 10000 at left in this photograph is Amtrak president, former secretary of the Navy, and former Southern Railway president W. Graham Claytor Jr. (Fred Clark Jr.)

Oops! The artist should have consulted *Webster's* prior to creating the placard on the front of Amtrak F40 locomotive 386. The misspelling—on signage celebrating the inaugural of the new Tampa-Miami *Silver Palm*—was corrected before the locomotive left Tampa Union Station on the premiere run of the new train the next day, November 20, 1982. (Joseph L. Oates.)

Flags flew on November 20, 1982, marking the premiere of a new Tampa-Miami passenger train, Amtrak's *Silver Palm*. The train—jointly financed by Amtrak and the Florida Department of Transportation and operated by Amtrak—was decorated that day with a placard affixed to the front of locomotive number 386, the earlier misspelling of the word "inaugural" having quickly been corrected. Number 386 is an F40 diesel-electric manufactured by the Electro-Motive Division of General Motors. (Fred Clark Jr.)

This photograph, taken from the observation platform of Amtrak office car 10000 on November 20, 1982, shows a crowd eagerly listening to dignitaries speaking on the occasion of the inaugural of the *Silver Palm*. Stops along the way for the Tampa-Miami train included Lakeland, Sebring, West Palm Beach, Delray Beach, and Fort Lauderdale. (Fred Clark Jr.)

Here, Amtrak's Tampa-Miami train *Silver Palm* heads out of Tampa Union Station and past the old Florida Brewing Company on September 22, 1984. An extra coach had been added to the train to accommodate passengers aboard the *Silver Palm Salvation Shuttle*, an event organized by WFLA radio personality and passenger train activist Jack Harris. State funding for the train had come under fire from Senate President Harry Johnston and others in the Florida Legislature who argued that state monies supporting the train's operation should be redirected to road-building. (Fred Clark Jr.)

In another view of the *Silver Palm* on the 1984 *Silver Palm Salvation Shuttle* run, the *Palm* heads out of Tampa Union Station behind F40 diesel-electric locomotive 382. Harris and others directed attention to the train's plight for a while, and the Florida Coalition of Railroad Passengers sued state government to stay the train's discontinuance, thereby managing to bring about a six-month extension of the train. Sadly, critics of the train ultimately prevailed, and operation of the train was halted in February 1985. Ironically, Amtrak revived the name *Silver Palm* for a New York–Florida service inaugurated in late 1996 as part of a service "realignment" which actually resulted in *less* train service to Florida's west coast. (Fred Clark Jr.)

Train time at Tampa Union Station during the Amtrak era is a very busy moment—just as it always has been for the terminal. On the morning of April 5, 1983, the north side of the station is abuzz with activity as passengers arrive to meet the *Silver Meteor*. Despite its age and deteriorating condition, the facility still effects a stately presence this day as a courtesy vehicle from the Ramada Inn North rushes to the front door of the building with a load of homeward-bound vacationers in a hurry to make their northbound train. (Nathan White Jr., courtesy Barbara Sharkey and Doug Rutledge.)

Here, passengers await their trains in the shade of the overhang trackside at Tampa Union Station, 1983. Note the old neon sign attached to the brick wall of the structure; it simply read "TAXICABS"; a neon arrow pointed the way to the cab stand under the building's port-cochere. (Courtesy of Special Collections, University of South Florida Library.)

In 1983, Amtrak passengers still purchased tickets for trains at the same ticket windows that had served the facility for most of its lifetime. The ticket office was relocated as part of the 1997–1998 renovation. (Courtesy of Special Collections, University of South Florida Library.)

Here, a General Motors–manufactured F40 diesel-electric locomotive waits patiently on the head of Amtrak's *Super Bowl Special* on January 22, 1984. Locomotive and train had made an express run from Washington D.C. to Tampa for the Super Bowl, played that year between the Washington Redskins and the Los Angeles Raiders at Tampa Stadium. The return trip to the nation's capital was less festive than the run south; Los Angeles won the game in a decisive victory. (Joseph L. Oates.)

Private railroad car Lehigh Valley 353 was photographed on the rear of Amtrak's *Silver Meteor* at Tampa Union Station on St. Patrick's Day, March 17, 1988. A former railroad office car once used by executives of the Lehigh Valley Railroad, the car was later owned by Dick Horstmann of Syracuse, New York. On this date, Horstmann's 353 was on the outbound segment of a Tampa-Savannah round-trip charter, carrying hearty revelers to Savannah's famous St. Patrick's Day festivities. A drumhead sign on the rear platform of the car honored one of the trains which had once traveled between Florida and points north—Seaboard Air Line's *Orange Blossom Special.* (Dudley C. Goodwin.)

In 1993, Amtrak and multinational conglomerate ABB sponsored a national tour of a high-speed Swedish trainset called the X2000. The futuristic train didn't leave Tampa off its itinerary, departing from Tampa Union Station's track 2 on several such demonstration runs in May of that year. The trainset—capable of speeds of up to 150 miles-per-hour—was actually on loan to Amtrak and its manufacturer ABB Traction by the Swedish national railway, SJ. (John McQuigg.)

Amtrak has now largely replaced the rag-tag, hand-me-down equipment it inherited from the nation's railroads at the time of its 1971 start-up; the vast majority of Amtrak cars and locomotives in service today were manufactured for the company in the 1980s and 1990s. In 1994, several members of a railroad passengers association inspected one of Amtrak's newest pieces of equipment, number 814. This P42 locomotive was manufactured by General Electric. (Andrew Healy.)

Today, General Electric Genesis-series diesel locomotives power the passenger trains that serve Tampa Union Station. Rated at 4,000 horsepower apiece, P42 locomotives like this one boast as features innovations which were unheard of in the station's early years, such as air-conditioned locomotive cabs and computerized controls. (Courtesy of Amtrak.)

By the 1990s, only two pieces of railroad equipment which had called on Tampa Union Station during the golden era of passenger rail could still be found dropping-by for an occasional visit. One of them was the former Seaboard Air Line Railroad ten-roomette, six-double-bedroom sleeping car "Sarasota," built for the railroad in 1949 by the Budd Company. In June 1994, it was at Tampa Union Station's Amtrak maintenance base for light work before it was returned to service. (Jackson McQuigg.)

Pictured here is Atlantic Coast Line Railroad steam locomotive 1639 on a passenger train near Tampa's Ybor City, during the late 1940s. Number 1639 was a 4-6-2 Pacific-type; engines of this wheel arrangement predominated on the main line railroads of the South during the 1920s, 1930s, and 1940s. (William J. Lenoir photograph, Jim Herron collection.)

The south side of Tampa Union Station and its adjacent parking lot are seen here as they appeared during the 1940s. (William J. Lenoir photograph, C.L. Goolsby collection.)

The station platforms at Union Station are seen here during the late 1950s or early 1960s. In much the same way as airports do, a day in the life of a train station during the glory years of passenger railroading alternated between bedlam and sheer quiet. Arriving and departing trains created wakes of frenetic activity; between train times, scenes could be just the opposite, as in this midday view. (William J. Lenoir photograph, Jim Herron collection.)

Atlantic Coast Line car 722 played a number of different roles all at once. Not only did the car contain a section for passenger baggage and Railway Express Agency parcels, but also a Railway Post Office section, where first-class mail and magazines were sorted en route by post office department employees. Number 722 is shown here at Tampa Union Station during the 1950s. (William J. Lenoir photograph, Jim Herron collection.)

Amtrak maintenance base and on-board services employees at Tampa Union Station were photographed on September 20, 1996. Hard-hatted assistant foreman-mechanical department Bill Rogers surveys the scene while on-board services supervisor Rudy Bautista and Dean Richie pass by on an electric cart. On November 10 of that year, these smiles would turn to frowns as, in a cost-cutting move, Amtrak shuttered the maintenance facility which it had occupied for just eight years. Amtrak employees were given the choice of moving to Miami or losing their jobs. (John McQuigg.)

A few members of the Florida Coalition of Railroad Passengers posed with Amtrak locomotive 270 after a rally at Tampa Union Station on November 10, 1996. Congressional budget cuts resulted in Amtrak's discontinuation of *Silver Star* service to Tampa that month, leaving the city with only two trains per day. For the first time in the station's history, railroad passengers found it impossible to travel between Tampa and Orlando by train. Amtrak has often had to defend its existence to Congressional critics—many of whom support millions for roads and airports, but object to funding Amtrak service, mistakenly believing that Amtrak trains are little used. Groups such as the Florida Coalition of Railroad Passengers disagree. (John McQuigg.)

This is an "oldie but goodie." Forever short on capital dollars, for much of the past 25 years Amtrak has had to make do with what was handed down to it from the days of private railroad-operated passenger service. The ten-roomette, six-double-bedroom sleeping car "Pine Island," shown here at Amtrak's maintenance base at Tampa Union Station in June 1995, was originally built in 1949 for the Atchison, Topeka & Santa Fe Railway by the Budd Company. (John McQuigg.)

103

In 1984, Amtrak elected to begin serving the cities of St. Petersburg and Clearwater through a dedicated bus connection, rather than directly by train. This necessitated moving Amtrak's maintenance base on Florida's west coast—hitherto located in St. Petersburg—across the bay to Tampa. The ultimate result was the 1988 construction of a $1-million maintenance base at Tampa Union Station. In October 1995, Amtrak sleeping car "Elm Grove" was shown at the

wheel-drop pit, its worn wheelsets being exchanged for new ones. Amtrak closed this facility on November 10, 1996, when, to save operating costs, new management decided to relocate all Amtrak Florida Service maintenance work to an older facility at Hialeah, Florida. (Jackson McQuigg.)

Shining stainless-steel Amtrak equipment glimmered in the late-afternoon sun on December 26, 1995, at Tampa Union Station. The cars at left await maintenance work at the carrier's maintenance facility at the station, while the cars on the right are spare coaches which can be put on a departing passenger train on short notice to accommodate unanticipated crowds or to replace a car taken out of service for mechanical reasons. (Jackson McQuigg.)

Amtrak not only ordered its own new passenger cars, but gave some older cars new leases on life, as well. The ten-roomette, six-double-bedroom sleeping car "Pacific Lodge" was built by the Budd Company for the Union Pacific Railroad in 1950. It is shown at Tampa Union Station on July 29, 1996, retired and stored with another old-timer after an incredible total of 46 years in revenue service. (Jackson McQuigg.)

Five

Rebirth

Concurrent with restoration work on the exterior of the building, workers descended on the inside of Tampa Union Station, replacing rotten wood, restoring plaster at the walls and cornice work, plumbing, re-wiring, re-glazing, adding a modern HVAC system, and performing a host of other tasks. The main waiting room is awash in Perry scaffolds and ladders as the camera finds artisans hard at work at their plastering trade. (Jim Herron.)

By November 1997, the exterior of Tampa Union Station was framed in scaffolding as masons began the tedious process of renewing and re-pointing the brick work on the building's exterior. First, the brick work was cleaned by means of a light sandblasting to remove the effects of decades of pollution and weather. Once the cleaning had been completed, a special blend of new Portland cement was added to replace missing and decayed mortar between the bricks. This process made it look as though years had been stripped from the building's age. (Jim Shephard.)

A long-disused office on the second floor of Tampa Union Station has been cleaned-up in this November 1997 photograph. Before restoration of the second-floor offices could begin in earnest, workers had to contend with collapsed plaster ceilings in these spaces. Thousands of cubic yards of ceiling plaster which had fallen from overhead and other debris had to be removed and disposed of. (Jim Herron.)

Restoration work on the exterior also included the rehabilitation and renewal of Tampa Union Station's famous arched windows. When restored, they were given several coats of dark green paint—a traditional railroad color which, during the restoration process, was found to be the historic appearance of the frames and associated millwork. (Jim Shephard.)

The magnitude of the rehabilitation which took place inside the station building is clearly evident in this November 1997 photograph. (Jim Herron.)

High atop a scaffold placed in the center of Tampa Union Station's main waiting room, a worker applies new framing to one of the station's skylights in November 1997. But unlike other Union Stations— Washington D.C.'s, for example—the skylights did not create a bright, light, airy feel inside of the main waiting room. Instead, the skylights filtered the light penetrating through them, creating a "moonglow" effect, according to architect Tom Hammer of Tampa's Rowe Architects, who headed-up the restoration. The historic look and feel of the skylights has been restored. (Jim Herron.)

Believe it or not, that plasterer's wheelbarrow is nowhere near the ground! A look through arched openings at a second-floor brick wall—stripped of its rotten plaster—yields a view of a worker on scaffolding high in the air. The waiting room and one of its overhead balconies can be seen behind the worker and platform. (Jim Herron.)

To facilitate their restoration work, employees of the general contractor set up a workshop in the former baggage building adjacent and connected to Tampa Union Station. This view shows two workers preparing window treatments for use in the building. (Jim Herron.)

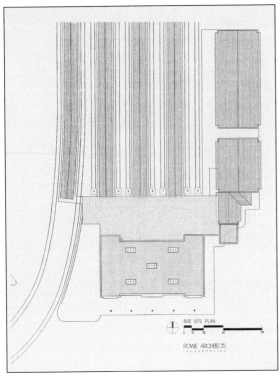

Here are the 1912 and 1997 site plans for Tampa Union Station. The 1997 plan shows the presence of two fewer active tracks, one fewer umbrella shed, and another major missing feature, the now-demolished express building. (Rowe Architects.)

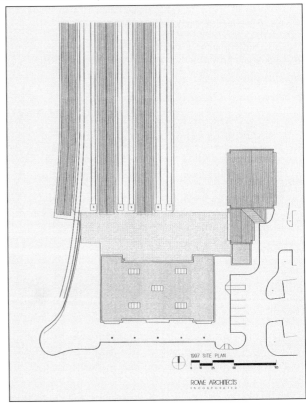

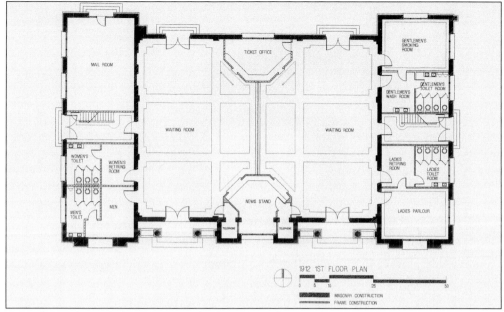

Main floor plans of the station for both 1912 and 1997 show not only substantial physical differences, but also the changing needs of railroad passengers during the course of an 85-year time span. Now gone are amenities such as the women's retiring room, the ladies' parlor, and the gentlemen's smoking room, replaced by such modern-day necessities as a vending area and a powered conveyor belt to handle passenger baggage. Also note how the location of the ticket office has changed from its original location in the post-restoration scheme. (Rowe Architects.)

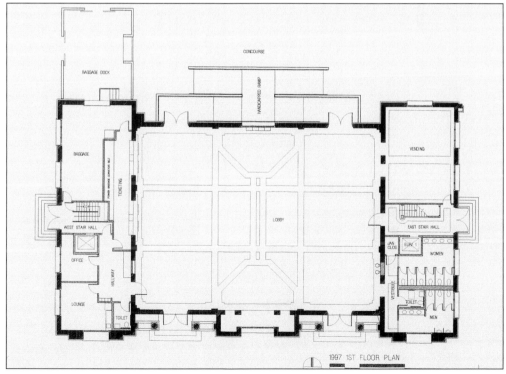

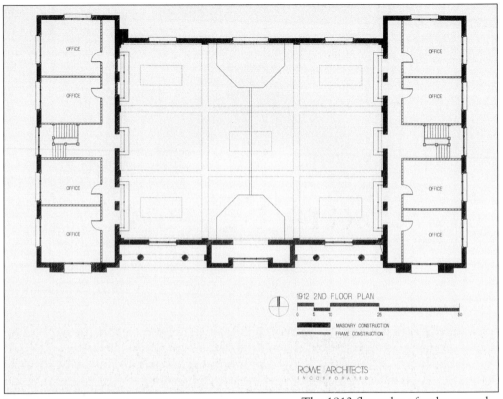

1912 2ND FLOOR PLAN

MASONRY CONSTRUCTION
FRAME CONSTRUCTION

ROWE ARCHITECTS
INCORPORATED

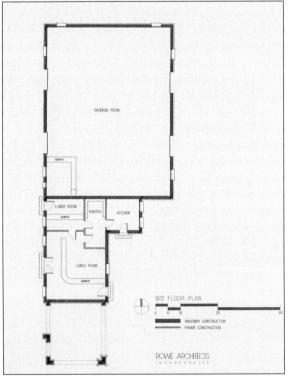

1912 FLOOR PLAN

MASONRY CONSTRUCTION
FRAME CONSTRUCTION

ROWE ARCHITECTS
INCORPORATED

The 1912 floor plans for the second floor, baggage room, and lunchroom area of Tampa Union Station are shown here. The baggage room continued to be used for its original function until Amtrak's ticketing and passenger functions vacated the station in 1984. The old lunchroom area was used as an Amtrak crew base in its later years. The crew base remained in the lunchroom until 1988. Meanwhile, offices, locker rooms, and other elements of the mechanical department—which was relocated from St. Petersburg when direct train service to that city was ended—resided in various portions of the station from 1984 until 1988. (Rowe Architects.)

Six
Extra Section

Adjacent to what is now the Kennedy Avenue (then Lafayette Street) bridge over the Hillsborough River downtown, Atlantic Coast Line Railroad employees in December 1932 built a Christmas garden for the enjoyment of the public. The garden, which was lighted at night, was located nearby the railroad's large freight depot on the last bank of the river. This scene photographed by Burgert Brothers, Commercial Photographers, shows that the garden came complete with a billboard offering greetings of the season to passersby. (Courtesy Tampa-Hillsborough County Public Library.)

While it doesn't show Tampa Union Station, this May 10, 1945 aerial view not only reflects the changing skyline of downtown Tampa, but also highlights two important landmarks of the Tampa railroad scene: the Cass Street railroad bridge over the Hillsborough River, which was on the Atlantic Coast Line main line heading out to Port Tampa (in the foreground), and the Atlantic Coast Line's freight depot and associated yards, in the upper right portion of the image. The railroad bridge and the Port Tampa railroad line are still in operation, but the freight depot was shuttered in the late 1950s.

Burgert Brothers, Commercial Photographers, captured these two women on October 28, 1947, enjoying the day on a bench in Plant Park, adjacent to the University of Tampa campus and the former Tampa Bay Hotel. While the women are engaged in conversation, the boy sitting on the river bank is clearly more interested in the Hillsborough River and the Atlantic Coast Line Railroad freight depot on the other side of it. In the distance, the Tampa skyline looms, including the Maas Brothers department store and Haverty Furniture. (Courtesy Tampa-Hillsborough County Public Library.)

Here's a March 17, 1926 aerial shot of Tampa's downtown, looking east. Business is booming at the Atlantic Coast Line Railroad freight depot in the foreground. Dozens of boxcars are on sidings adjacent to the sheds waiting to be loaded or unloaded. (Courtesy Tampa-Hillsborough County Public Library.)

Atlantic Coast Line operated a small facility for off-loading new automobiles arriving in the city. A number of boxcars specially equipped to transport new automobiles are visible in this August 30, 1929 view of the facility, which was located in downtown Tampa nearby O. Falk's department store. J.E. Burgert took this photograph—probably for the Coast Line's law department—after a highway grade-crossing accident took place at the site. (Courtesy Tampa-Hillsborough County Public Library.)

While its trains never used Tampa Union Station directly, Tampa-based Royal American Shows did its part to encourage travelers to put the Cigar City on their lists of places to visit. On April 1, 1946, Royal American Shows' car 56 was pictured at the railroad yard adjacent to the Florida State Fairgrounds in Tampa, resplendent in a hand-painted scheme promoting tourism to the city. This was no small boon to the city, for in the 1940s, Royal American boasted the world's largest midway, employed for a time famous stripper Gypsy Rose Lee, and witnessed its founder, Carl J. Sedlmayr, portrayed on the silver screen thanks to a major Hollywood motion picture about his life. (Courtesy Tampa-Hillsborough County Public Library.)

Some New Deal programs even helped out the railroads. In 1933, labor crews of the Tampa Emergency Relief Council work on the Platt Street railroad crossing near the Seaboard Air Line Railway's Tampa Yard, not too far from Tampa Union Station. (Courtesy Tampa-Hillsborough County Public Library.)

Atlantic Coast Line 4-6-2 Pacific-type steam locomotive 1504 is shown here at UCETA Yard, Tampa, on June 1, 1956. This locomotive—which once pulled famous Coast Line passenger trains such as the *Havana Special*—was destined for preservation when this photograph was made. Within four years the locomotive would be proudly displayed in front of the Atlantic Coast Line Railroad headquarters building in Jacksonville, Florida, thanks to railroad president W.T. Rice and his predecessor, Champion McDowell Davis. (M.D. McCarter photograph collection, N3530A.)

Like its sister facility in St. Petersburg, the facility Amtrak used in Lakeland was built by the Atlantic Coast Line Railroad in the early 1960s, and, again like the St. Petersburg station, the facility was built as a combination freight-passenger depot. Unlike St. Petersburg, the Lakeland station kept direct train service until 1998, when it was replaced by a brand-new structure on Lake Mirror downtown. The 1960s classic still looked respectable however, in this August 7, 1995 image. (Jackson McQuigg.)

Here is Seaboard Air Line's St. Petersburg station in a 1948 photograph taken by Harry A. McBride. The station—located at Second Avenue, South, and at Ninth Street, South—was virtually surrounded by the famous Webb's City drugstore. Tracks of both the Seaboard and its rival, Atlantic Coast Line, actually ran right down the middle of city streets to get to their respective depots downtown; trains stopped at these stations to board or discharge passengers—at the Seaboard station, particularly—tended to snarl automobile traffic. Frustrated by this, local government urged both railroads to move their stations out of the city center. Seaboard eventually complied and closed this station in June 1963. (Smithsonian Institution.)

This is a trackside view of the 1960s-built Coast Line and Amtrak station at Lakeland. Platform canopies were constructed of concrete—a far different material than the wood used to frame those at Tampa Union Station. (Jackson McQuigg.)

The old Seaboard Air Line Tampa Yard is still used at times. On December 24, 1994, one of the two units of the Ringling Brothers and Barnum & Bailey Circus spent the Christmas holiday at the yard. A string of grain hopper cars waits patiently for their turn at the ConAgra bakery flour elevators at adjacent Finley and Alma Streets. In the background, from left to right, are the Florida Aquarium, Tampa Electric Hooker's Point power plant, and the Garrison Channel cruise ship terminal, with the Russian cruise ship *Gruzya* in port. (Jackson McQuigg.)

The former Atlantic Coast Line, Seaboard Coast Line, and Amtrak station at St. Petersburg is shown here. Direct train service to the station at 3601 Thirty-first Street, North was ended by Amtrak in February 1984; the bus service was relocated to a new location at Pinellas Square Mall in June 1995. Left to rack and ruin, the station appeared forlorn on August 6, 1995, with a heavy overgrowth of weeds where tracks had once been. The building has since been acquired by a health care company. (Jackson McQuigg.)

One of the most distinctive freight locomotive types on the Seaboard Air Line Railroad roster was the Baldwin "centipede"-type, which featured no less than 12 wheelsets. Centipede 4504 is shown here at Tampa Yard during the 1950s along with a smaller, Electro-Motive Division–manufactured counterpart. Despite its size, the technology behind the design of 4504 and her sisters soon became obsolete; this locomotive was retired by the end of 1957, having stayed just ten years in on the railroad's roster. Tampa Union Station is visible at the top of the photograph. (J.M. Gruber collection via Joseph L. Oates.)

Sometimes Seaboard Air Line Railway stored passenger equipment—temporarily idle and removed from the house tracks at Tampa Union Station—in the road's nearby yard, Tampa Yard. Thus, commercial photographer J.E. Burgert found a Seaboard baggage car waiting for its next assignment on April 26, 1930, while steam locomotive 1119 prepares to couple onto a string of phosphate cars headed for the railroad-owned, rail-ship facility at Seddon Island. This spectacular view required a bit of bravery on the part of the photographer—it was taken from the rooftop walkway of a freight car. (J.E. Burgert photograph, Joseph L. Oates collection.)

Seaboard Air Line Railroad steam locomotive 929 was photographed at Tampa Yard in the late 1940s or early 1950s. The 929—a switch engine—was assigned to shuffle cars around the busy yard. The roof line of Tampa Union Station is clearly visible in the background, just over the tops of several adjacent buildings. (William J. Lenoir photograph, Atlantic Coast Line and Seaboard Air Line Railroads Historical Society collection.)

This is Seaboard Air Line Railroad's Tampa Yard in the late 1940s or early 1950s. This once-busy yard—roughly bordered by Meridian, Cumberland, Platt, Twiggs, and Brush Streets in the Garrison Seaport district—still exists in 1997, though it is largely disused. But at the time this photograph was taken showing some of the road's steam and diesel-electric locomotives and cabooses, it was Seaboard's main yard in Tampa. Behind a stockyard and on the other side of Twiggs Street, Tampa Union Station faces downtown, beckoning travelers to its doors—just as it has done for decades. (William J. Lenoir photograph, Atlantic Coast Line and Seaboard Air Line Railroads Historical Society collection.)

Shown here are the UCETA Shops, Tampa, 1950s. Steam and diesel-electric locomotives for both passenger and freight trains were overhauled at this Atlantic Coast Line repair facility east of the city. The backshop—the building in which heavy overhauls of locomotives took place—is pictured in the background here, while diesel-electric locomotive 335 idles next to a Coast Line steam engine. By the end of the decade, steam engines would be stricken from the railroad's equipment roster, having been replaced in their entirety by the more efficient diesels. (William J. Lenoir photograph, Jim Herron collection.)

Atlantic Coast Line steam locomotive 829 passes the southern edge of the Tampa Union Station property with a train of oil tankers during World War II. Headed for Port Tampa, 829 and her train represented an important part of the war effort. Coastwise shipping was severely disrupted by German U-boat activity during the war. The burden of transporting petroleum products around the nation thus fell to the railroads—who responded to the challenge with an impressive and resourceful might. (William J. Lenoir photograph, Jim Herron collection.)

Diesel-electric switcher locomotive 648 was regularly assigned to switch not only Atlantic Coast Line equipment at Tampa Union Station, but also the Coast Line freight sheds on the western end of downtown. This Atlantic Coast Line locomotive was a veritable fixture of Tampa railroading during the 1950s. The SW7-model locomotive was delivered to the Coast Line from the Electro-Motive Division of General Motors in 1950 in an eye-catching purple, silver, and gold paint scheme—standard for all of the railroad's diesel locomotives at the time—which it wore until the 1960s. (William J. Lenoir photograph, Jim Herron collection.)

Here, UCETA Shops at Tampa are shown as they appeared during the 1950s. Atlantic Coast Line steam and diesel-electric locomotives, and passenger and freight cars were all repaired at UCETA Shops during its heyday. Locomotive 1695 was a 4-6-2 Pacific-type steam locomotive built by the Baldwin Locomotive Works for use on Coast Line passenger trains. It is shown pulling onto the turntable at the UCETA Shops' roundhouse. In the background, workers are giving the steam locomotive's nemesis—one of the new diesel-electrics—a bath. (William J. Lenoir photograph, Jim Herron collection.)

Just out of the paint shop at the West Jacksonville Shops in Jacksonville, Florida, in 1971 is motor car 4900, which was originally built for Seaboard Coast Line Railroad predecessor Seaboard Air Line. 4900—a combination locomotive-and-baggage car unit—frequented Tampa Union Station right up until the advent of Amtrak in May 1971. Unfortunately, and despite efforts to the contrary, neither 4900 nor her sister were preserved; both met the scrapper's torch later that same year. (Seaboard Coast Line photograph, Jim Herron collection.)

The facility which Amtrak used at St. Pete during the 1970s and 1980s was fairly new by railroad standards, having been built by the Atlantic Coast Line Railroad in the early 1960s. By 1984, Amtrak had decided that it could better and more cheaply serve the passengers of St. Petersburg and Clearwater by sending chartered busses from Tampa to the stations in these cities. In 1995, with the establishment of a bus stop and ticket counter at Pinellas Square Mall, Amtrak abandoned the two railroad stations altogether. The St. Pete station was still going strong in June 1974, however, when an Amtrak train in the capable charge of SDP40F locomotive 549 was captured on film. (Jim Herron.)

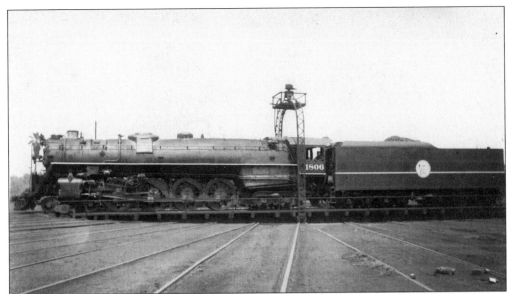

Atlantic Coast Line Railroad steam locomotive 1806 was built by the Baldwin Locomotive Works for fast Coast Line passenger trains. The mammoth engine of the 4-8-4 wheel arrangement is pictured on the turntable at the UCETA Shops roundhouse in Tampa during the 1950s. While not regularly used on passenger trains emanating from Tampa, these locomotives were routinely overhauled at the once-bustling railroad repair shop here. (William J. Lenoir photo, Jim Herron collection.)

This is the old Atlantic Coast Line Railroad St. Petersburg station at First Avenue, South, at Second Street, South, downtown in a postcard view from the 1920s. This classic structure was replaced by the more mundane 1963 station that was later used by Amtrak. The new station would be located on the north side of the city. (Author's collection.)